BREAD MACHINE

*To Prepare Simple and Easy Recipes for
Making a Great Bread at Home*

SARAH BETH

Table of Contents

Sommario

Introduction

Here's why your kitchen needs a bread machine

With a handy bread machine, you can make homemade bread and other dough-based preparations in just a few hours.

If you love the taste, smell, and texture of freshly baked bread - especially when it's homemade - you need to have a bread machine among your kitchen tools.

Everything a bread machine can do

Many bread machines on the market can make a 2 lb loaf of crispy, chewy, soft bread. Best of all, it does all the work for you.

A bread machine is capable of making more than just a regular loaf of bread. The preparation possibilities are endless once you get the hang of working with it. It can be used to make countless appetizers, side dishes, and meals, from gooey cinnamon rolls to soft dinner rolls, from Indian-style naan to Belgian-style soft pretzels, and every doughy recipe in between.

Most bread machines come with a kneading function, which can be used to knead the dough, pizza, and more. You can even bake a warm, moist cake in a bread machine.

Bread machines cook at a fairly low temperature, which makes them great for making many dishes that can typically be done in a slow cooker. It has several features that can be used for a variety of recipes. You can also make jams, as well as sauces, stews, soups, even scrambled eggs and yogurt.

To help spur your creations, we've grouped a few dozen tasty recipes that you can use with a bread machine.

Spiced Jalapeno Cheese Bread

Servings: 1 Pound Loaf

Cooking Time: 3 Hours

Ingredients:
Lukewarm water :½ cup
Milk powder :2 tbsp
Unsalted butter :2 tbsp
Plain bread flour :1 ½ cup
Cheddar cheese :½ cup
Jalapeno pepper, finely diced :½
Granulated brown sugar :1 tbsp
Salt :1 tsp
Bread machine yeast :¾ tsp

Directions:
Combine the water and instant milk powder first, then add it to your bread machine.
Add the remaining ingredients into the bread machine as per the order of the ingredients listed above or follow your bread machine's instruction manual.
Select the basic setting and soft crust function.
When ready, turn the bread out onto a drying rack and allow it to cool, then serve.

Nutrition Info: Calories: 135 kcal / Total fat: 4.9 g / Saturated fat: 3 g / Cholesterol: 14 mg / Total carbohydrates: 18.1 g / Dietary fiber: 0.7g / Sodium: 327 mg / Protein: 4.6 g

Sourdough

Servings: 1 Pound Loaf

Cooking Time: 3 Hours

Ingredients:
for a sourdough starter:
2 cups white, all-purpose flour
1 tsp active dry yeast
2 cups lukewarm water for bread
Sourdough starter :½ cup
Lukewarm water :⅓ cup
Sugar :½ tbsp
Active dry yeast :½ tbsp
Plain bread flour :1 ½ cups
Vegetable oil :1 ½ tbsp
Salt :1 tsp

Directions:

for a sourdough starter:

Combine the ingredients in a glass or ceramic dish. Ensure the dish is big enough to allow for expansion. Cover the dish with cloth, fix the cloth into place using an elastic band.

Allow the starter to rest for five days in a warm area. Stir the starter once a day.

Your starter sourdough is now ready for use. Refrigerate the remainder and use it when needed. If you would like to make a few loaves, you can keep the sourdough starter "alive" by feeding it equal amounts of flour and water and allowing it to rest in a warm area and using it when needed.

for bread:

Add the sourdough starter, water, sugar, and yeast into the bread maker. Using a spatula, combine the ingredients. Allow it to rest for ten minutes.

Add bread flour, oil, and salt. Select the basic setting and medium crust function.

When ready, turn the bread out onto a drying rack and allow it to cool, then serve.

Nutrition Info: Calories: 181.3 kcal / Total fat: 4.5 g / Saturated fat: 0.6 g Cholesterol: 0 mg / Total carbohydrates: 30.4 g / Dietary fiber: 1.3 g / Sodium: 467 mg / Protein: 4.4 g

Seeded Whole Wheat Bread

Servings: 1 Pound Loaf

Cooking Time: 3 Hours

Ingredients:
Lukewarm water :⅔ cups
Milk powder :3 tbsp
Honey :1 tbsp
Unsalted butter, softened :1 tbsp
Plain bread flour :1 cup
Whole wheat flour :1 cup
Poppy seeds :2 tbsp
Sesame seeds :2 tbsp
Sunflower seeds :2 tbsp
Salt :¾ tsp
Instant dry yeast :2 tsp

Directions:
Add the ingredients into the bread machine as per the order of the
ingredients listed above or follow your bread machine's instruction
manual.
Select the basic setting and medium crust function.
When ready, turn the bread out onto a drying rack and allow it to cool,
then serve.

Nutrition Info: (Per Serving):Calories: 84 kcal / Total fat: 2 g /
Saturated fat: 1 g / Cholesterol: 2 mg / Total carbohydrates: 14 g /
Dietary fiber: 1 g Sodium: 133 mg / Protein: 3 g

Breakfast Bread

Servings: 16 Slices

Cooking Time: 40 Minutes

Ingredients:
½ tsp. Xanthan gum
½ tsp. salt
2 Tbsp. coconut oil
½ cup butter, melted
tsp. baking powder
cups of almond flour   Seven eggs

Directions:
Preheat the oven to 355F.
Beat eggs in a bowl on high for 2 minutes.
Add coconut oil and butter to the eggs and continue to beat.
Line a pan with baking paper and then pour the beaten eggs.
Pour in the rest of the ingredients and mix until it becomes thick.
Bake until a toothpick comes out dry. It takes 40 to 45 minutes.

Nutrition Info: Calories: 234 ;Fat: 23g ;Carb: 1g;Protein: 7g ;

Apple Butter Bread

Servings: 1 Loaf

Cooking Time: 10 Minutes Plus Fermenting Time

Ingredients:
8 slices bread (1 pound)
⅔ cup milk, at 80°F to 90°F
⅓ cup apple butter, at room temperature
4 teaspoons melted butter, cooled
2 teaspoons honey
⅔ teaspoon salt
⅔ cup whole-wheat flour
1½ cups white bread flour
1 teaspoon bread machine or instant yeast

Directions:
Preparing the Ingredients.
Choose the size of loaf of your preference and then measure the ingredients.
Add all of the ingredients mentioned previously in the list.
Close the lid after placing the pan in the bread machine.
Select the Bake cycle
Turn on the bread machine. Select the Quick/Rapid setting, select the loaf size, and the crust color. Press start.
When the cycle is finished, carefully remove the pan from the bread maker and let it rest.
Remove the bread from the pan, put in a wire rack to Cool about 5 minutes. Slice

Onion And Cheese Bread

Servings: 12

Cooking Time: 3 Hours And 25 Minutes

Ingredients:
Lukewarm water - ¾ cup
Wheat bread flour - 3 2/3 cups
Cottage cheese - ¾ cup
Butter - 2 tbsp., softened
White sugar - 2 tbsp.
Sea salt - 1½ tsp.
Sesame seeds - 1½ tbsp.
Dried onions - 2 tbsp.
Bread machine yeast - 1¼ tsp.

Directions:
Place everything in the bread pan according to bread machine recommendations.
Select Basic and Medium crust.
Remove the bread when done.
Cool, slice, and serve.

Nutrition Info: (Per Serving): Calories: 277; Total Fat: 4.7 g; Saturated Fat: 2.3 g; Carbohydrates: 48.4 g; Cholesterol: 9 mg; Fiber: 1.9 g; Calcium: 41 mg; Sodium: 547 mg; Protein: 9.4 g

Vanilla Almond Milk Bread

Servings: 1 Loaf

Cooking Time: 10 Minutes Plus Fermenting Time

Ingredients:
12 slice bread (1½ pounds)
½ cup plus 1 tablespoon milk, at 80°F to 90°F
3 tablespoons melted butter, cooled
3 tablespoons sugar
1 egg, at room temperature
1½ teaspoons pure vanilla extract
⅓ teaspoon almond extract
2½ cups white bread flour
1½ teaspoons bread machine or instant yeast

Directions:
Preparing the Ingredients.
Choose the size of loaf of your preference and then measure the ingredients.
Add all of the ingredients mentioned previously in the list.
Close the lid after placing the pan in the bread machine.
Select the Bake cycle
Turn on the bread machine. Select the Sweet setting, select the loaf size, and the crust color. Press start.
When the cycle is finished, carefully remove the pan from the bread maker and let it rest.
Remove the bread from the pan, put in a wire rack to Cool about 5 minutes. Slice

Everyday Fruit Bread

Servings: 15

Cooking Time: 3 Hours And 25 Minutes

Ingredients:
Egg – 1
Water – 1 cup, plus 2 tbsp.
Ground cardamom – ½ tsp.
Salt – 1 tsp.
Sugar – 1 ½ tbsp.
Butter – ¼ cup
Bread flour – 3 cups
Bread machine yeast – 1 tsp.
Raisins – 1/3 cup
Mixed candied fruit – 1/3 cup

Directions:
Place all ingredients (except fruit and raisins) in the bread machine according to machine recommendation.
Select Basic White or Fruit and Nut setting.
Add the fruit and raisins after the beep.
When finished, remove the bread.
Cool, slice, and serve.

Nutrition Info: (Per Serving): Calories: 144; Total Fat: 3.6 g; Saturated Fat: 2.1 g; Carbohydrates: 24.6 g; Cholesterol: 19 mg; Fiber: 1 g; Calcium: 9 mg; Sodium: 183 mg; Protein: 3.2 g

Peaches And Cream Bread

Servings: 1 Loaf

Cooking Time: 10 Minutes

Ingredients:
12 slice bread (1½ pounds)
¾ cup canned peaches, drained and chopped
⅓ cup heavy whipping cream, at 80°F to 90°F
1 egg, at room temperature
1 tablespoon melted butter, cooled
2¼ tablespoons sugar
1⅛ teaspoons salt
⅓ teaspoon ground cinnamon
⅛ teaspoon ground nutmeg
⅓ cup whole-wheat flour
2⅔ cups white bread flour
1⅛ teaspoons bread machine or instant yeast

Directions:
Preparing the Ingredients.
Choose the size of loaf of your preference and then measure the ingredients.
Add all of the ingredients mentioned previously in the list. Close the lid after placing the pan in the bread machine.
Select the Bake cycle
Turn on the bread machine. Select the White/Basic setting, select the loaf size, and the crust color. Press start.
When the cycle is finished, carefully remove the pan from the bread maker and let it rest.
Remove the bread from the pan, put in a wire rack to Cool completely, about 10 minutes.

Savory Sweet Potato Pan Bread

Servings: 1 Loaf

Cooking Time: 10 Minutes

Ingredients:
8 wedges
1½ cups uncooked shredded dark-orange sweet potato
(about ½ potato)
½ cup sugar
¼ cup vegetable oil
2 eggs
¾ cup all-purpose flour
¾ cup whole wheat flour
2 teaspoons dried minced onion
1 teaspoon dried rosemary leaves, crumbled
teaspoon baking soda
½ teaspoon salt
¼ teaspoon baking powder
teaspoons sesame seed

Directions:
Preparing the Ingredients.
Choose the size of loaf of your preference and then measure the
ingredients. Add all of the ingredients mentioned previously in the list.
Close the lid after placing the pan in the bread machine.
Select the Bake cycle Turn on the bread machine. Select the
White/Basic setting, select the loaf size, and the crust color. Press start.
When the cycle is finished, carefully remove the pan from the bread
maker and let it rest.
Remove the bread from the pan, put in a wire rack to Cool about 10
minutes. Serve warm.

Pineapple Coconut Bread

Servings: 1 Loaf

Cooking Time: 10 Minutes

Ingredients:
6 tablespoons butter, at room temperature
2 eggs, at room temperature
½ cup coconut milk, at room temperature
½ cup pineapple juice, at room temperature
cup sugar
1½ teaspoons coconut extract
cups all-purpose flour
¾ cup shredded sweetened coconut
1 teaspoon baking powder
½ teaspoon salt

Directions:
Preparing the Ingredients.
Place the butter, eggs, coconut milk, pineapple juice, sugar, and coconut extract in your bread machine.
Program the machine for Quick/Rapid bread and press Start.
While the wet ingredients are mixing, stir together the flour, coconut, baking powder, and salt in a small bowl.
Select the Bake cycle
After the first fast mixing is done and the machine signals, add the dry ingredients.
When the cycle is finished, carefully remove the pan from the bread maker and let it rest. 8.   Remove the bread from the pan, put in a wire rack to cool for at least 10 minutes, and slice.

Cheese Onion Garlic Bread

Servings: 10

Cooking Time: 3 Hours

Ingredients:
Cheddar cheese – 1 cup., shredded   Dried onion – 3 tbsps., minced
Garlic powder – 2 tsps.
Active dry yeast – 2 tsps.
Margarine – 2 tbsps.
Sugar – 2 tbsps.
Milk Powder – 2 tbsps.
Bread flour – 3 cups.
Warm water – 1 1/8 cups.
Salt – 1 ½ tsps.

Directions:
Add water, salt, flour, milk powder, sugar, margarine, and yeast into the bread machine pan. Select basic setting then select medium crust and press start. Add cheese, dried onion, and garlic powder just before the final kneading cycle. Once loaf is done, remove the loaf pan from the machine. Allow it to cool for 10 minutes. Slice and serve.

Almond Milk Bread

Servings: 1 Loaf

Ingredients:
16 slice bread (2 pounds)
cup lukewarm milk
eggs, at room temperature
2⅔ tablespoons butter, melted and cooled
⅓ cup sugar
1 teaspoon table salt
2⅓ teaspoons lemon zest
4 cups white bread flour
2¼ teaspoons bread machine yeast
½ cup slivered almonds, chopped
½ cup golden raisins, chopped
12 slice bread (1½ pounds)
¾ cup lukewarm milk
2 eggs, at room temperature
2 tablespoons butter, melted and cooled
¼ cup sugar
teaspoon table salt
teaspoons lemon zest
cups white bread flour
2 teaspoons bread machine yeast
⅓ cup slivered almonds, chopped
⅓ cup golden raisins, chopped

Directions:

Choose the size of loaf you would like to make and measure your ingredients.

Add all of the ingredients except for the raisins and almonds to the bread pan in the order listed above.

Place the pan in the bread machine and close the lid.

Turn on the bread maker. Select the White/Basic or Fruit/Nut (if your machine has this setting) setting, then the loaf size, and finally the crust color. Start the cycle.

When the machine signals to add ingredients, add the raisins and almonds. (Some machines have a fruit/nut hopper where you can add the raisins and almonds when you start the machine. The machine will automatically add them to the dough during the baking process.)

When the cycle is finished and the bread is baked, carefully remove the pan from the machine. Use a potholder as the handle will be very hot. Let rest for a few minutes.

Remove the bread from the pan and allow to cool on a wire rack for at least 10 minutes before slicing.

Nutrition Info: Calories 193, fat 4.6 g, carbs 29.4 g, sodium 214 mg, protein 5.7 g

Tuscan Herb Bread

Servings: 10

Cooking Time: 2 Hours

Ingredients:
Yeast – 2 tsps.
Bread flour – 2 1/2 cups
Italian seasoning – 2 tbsps.
Sugar – 2 tbsps.
Olive oil – 2 tbsps.
Warm water – 1 cup
Salt – 1 tsp.

Directions:
Add olive oil and water to the bread pan. Add remaining ingredients except for yeast to the bread pan. Make a small hole into the flour with your finger and add yeast to the hole. Make sure yeast will not be mixed with any liquids. Select basic setting then select light/medium crust and start. Once loaf is done, remove the loaf pan from the machine. Allow it to cool for 10 minutes. Slice and serve.

Lavender Buttermilk Bread

Servings: 14 Slices

Cooking Time: 3 H.

Ingredients:
½ cup water
⅞ cup buttermilk
¼ cup olive oil
3 Tbsp finely chopped fresh lavender leaves
1 ¼ tsp finely chopped fresh lavender flowers
Grated zest of 1 lemon
4 cups bread flour
2 tsp salt
2 ¾ tsp bread machine yeast

Directions:
Add each ingredient to the bread machine in the order and at the temperature recommended by your bread machine manufacturer. Close the lid, select the basic bread, medium crust setting on your bread machine and press start.
When the bread machine has finished baking, remove the bread and put it on a cooling rack.

Herbed Pesto Bread

Servings: 1 Loaf

Cooking Time: 10 Minutes

Ingredients:
12 slices bread (1½ pounds)
1 cup water, at 80°F to 90°F
2¼ tablespoons melted butter, cooled
1½ teaspoons minced garlic
¾ tablespoon sugar
1 teaspoon salt
3 tablespoons chopped fresh parsley
1½ tablespoons chopped fresh basil
⅓ cup grated Parmesan cheese
3 cups white bread flour
1¼ teaspoons bread machine or active dry yeast

Directions:
Preparing the Ingredients.
Choose the size of loaf of your preference and then measure the ingredients.
Add all of the ingredients mentioned previously in the list.
Close the lid after placing the pan in the bread machine.
Select the Bake cycle
Turn on the bread machine. Select the White/Basic setting, select the loaf size, and the crust color. Press start.
When the cycle is finished, carefully remove the pan from the bread maker and let it rest.
Remove the bread from the pan, put in a wire rack to Cool about 10 minutes. Slice

Finnish Pulla

Servings: 1 Loaf

Cooking Time: 30 Minutes

Ingredients:
1 cup milk
1/4 cup water, lukewarm
eggs, 1 egg reserved for glaze
1/2 cups all purpose flour
1/2 cup sugar
1 teaspoon salt
1 tablespoon ground cardamom
tablespoon yeast
1/4 cup butter, cut into 4 chunks
1-2 tablespoons pearl sugar for topping loaves

Directions:

Place the milk, water, and 2 lightly beaten eggs in bread machine pan. Add flour, sugar, salt, cardamom in the pan, then top it with yeast and butter. Program the bread machine to dough setting.

Remove the dough from the bread machine pan and place on a lightly floured surface. Divide the dough into 3 equal pieces. Roll each piece of dough into 10-14 inch strand and braid. Pinch and tuck the ends under and place on greased or parchment covered baking sheet. Lightly cover it with a clean kitchen towel and let it rise for about 30-45 minutes.

Preheat the oven to 325 degrees. Beat the remaining egg and gently brush the loaf on top and on the sides with pastry brush. Sprinkle with pearl sugar. Bake for 20 to 25 minutes until it becomes light golden brown. Cool on wire rack, then slice to serve.

Nutrition Info: Total Fat 4.5g; Saturated fat 2.5g; Cholesterol 35mg; Sodium 140mg; Carbohydrates 26g; Net carbs 25g;Sugar 5g; Fiber 1g;Protein 4g

Fiji Sweet Potato Bread

Servings: 1 Loaf

Cooking Time: 1 Hour And 10minutes

Ingredients:
One teaspoon vanilla extract
½ cup of warm water
4 cups flour
1 cup sweet mashed potatoes
Two tablespoons softened butter
½ teaspoon cinnamon
1 ½ teaspoons salt
1/3 cup brown sugar
Two tablespoons powdered milk
Two teaspoons yeast

Directions:
Add everything in the pan of your bread.
Select the white bread and the crust you want.
Hit the start button.
Set aside on wire racks for cooling before slicing.

Nutrition Info: Calories: 168 Cal; Carbohydrates: 28 g;
Fat: 5g;Cholesterol: 0 mg; Protein: 4 g; Fiber: 1g; Sugat 3 g;
Sodium: 292 mg

Butter Bread

Servings: 1 Pound Loaf

Cooking Time: 3 Hours And 35 Minutes

Ingredients:
Egg :1
Lukewarm whole milk :1 ¼ cup
Unsalted butter, diced :½ cup
Plain bread flour :2 cups
Salt :1 pinch
Sugar :1 pinch
Instant dry yeast :2 tsp

Directions:
Add the ingredients into the bread machine as per the order of the ingredients listed above or follow your bread machine's instruction manual.
Select the French setting and medium crust function.
When ready, turn the bread out onto a drying rack and allow it to cool, then serve.

Nutrition Info: Calories: 262.2 kcal / Total fat: 13.5 g / Saturated fat: 8.2 g / Cholesterol: 58.6 mg / Total carbohydrates 29.8 g / Dietary fiber: 1.3 g / Sodium: 45.3 mg / Protein: 5.9 g

Cashew Butter/peanut Butter Bread

Servings: 1 Loaf

Cooking Time: 10 Minutes Plus Fermenting Time

Ingredients:
12 slice bread (1½ pounds)
1 cup peanut butter or cashew butter
1 cup lukewarm milk
½ cup packed light brown sugar
¼ cup sugar
¼ cup butter, at room temperature
egg, at room temperature
teaspoons pure vanilla extract
2 cups all-purpose flour
1 tablespoon baking powder
½ teaspoon table salt

Directions:
Preparing the Ingredients.
Choose the size of loaf of your preference and then measure the ingredients. Add all of the ingredients mentioned previously in the list. Close the lid after placing the pan in the bread machine.
Select the Bake cycle
Turn on the bread machine. Select the Quick/Rapid setting, select the loaf size, and the crust color. Press start.
When the cycle is finished, carefully remove the pan from the bread maker and let it rest.
Remove the bread from the pan, put in a wire rack to Cool about 5 minutes. Slice

Sweet Banana Bread

Servings: 10

Cooking Time: 2 Hours

Ingredients:
Warm milk – ½ cup.
Vanilla extract – 1 tsp.
Butter – 8 tbsps.
Eggs – 2
Salt – ½ tsp.
All-purpose flour – 2 cups.
Sugar – 1 cup.
Bananas – 3, mashed
Baking soda – 1 tsp.
Baking powder – 2 tsps.

Directions:
Add all ingredients into the bread machine pan. Select quick bread setting then select light crust and press start. Once loaf is done, remove the loaf pan from the machine. Allow it to cool for 10 minutes. Slice and serve.

Cranberry-cornmeal Bread

Servings: 1 Loaf

Cooking Time: 10 Minutes Plus Fermenting Time

Ingredients:
12 slice bread (1½ pounds)
1 cup plus 1 tablespoon water
3 tablespoons molasses or honey
tablespoons butter, softened
cups bread flour
1/3 cup cornmeal
1½ teaspoons salt
2 teaspoons bread machine yeast
½ cup sweetened dried cranberries

Directions:
Preparing the Ingredients.
Choose the size of loaf of your preference and then measure the
ingredients. Add all of the ingredients mentioned previously in the list
except cranberries Close the lid after placing the pan in the bread
machine. Add cranberries at the Raisin/Nut signal or 5 to 10 minutes
before last kneading cycle ends.
Select the Bake cycle Program the machine for White/Basic bread and
press Start. After the first fast mixing is done, add the flour, coconut,
cinnamon, baking soda, baking powder, nutmeg, ginger, and allspice.
When the cycle is finished, carefully remove the pan from the bread
maker and let it rest.
Remove the bread from the pan, put in a wire rack to Cool about 5
minutes. Slice.

Strawberry Shortcake Bread

Servings: 1 Loaf

Cooking Time: 10 Minutes

Ingredients:
12 slice bread (1½ pounds)
1⅛ cups milk, at 80°F to 90°F
3 tablespoons melted butter, cooled
3 tablespoons sugar
1½ teaspoons salt
¾ cup sliced fresh strawberries
1 cup quick oats
2¼ cups white bread flour
1½ teaspoons bread machine or instant yeast

Directions:
Preparing the Ingredients.
Choose the size of loaf of your preference and then measure the ingredients.
Add all of the ingredients mentioned previously in the list. Close the lid after placing the pan in the bread machine.
Select the Bake cycle
Turn on the bread machine. Select the White/Basic setting, select the loaf size, and the crust color. Press start.
When the cycle is finished, carefully remove the pan from the bread maker and let it rest.
Remove the bread from the pan, put in a wire rack to cool for at least 2 hours, and slice.

Cranberry & Golden Raisin Bread

Servings: 14 Slices

Cooking Time: 10 Minutes

Ingredients:
1⅓ cups water
4 Tbsp sliced butter
3 cups flour
1 cup old fashioned oatmeal
⅓ cup brown sugar
1 tsp salt
4 Tbsp dried cranberries
4 Tbsp golden raisins
2 tsp bread machine yeast

Directions:
Preparing the Ingredients
Add each ingredient except cranberries and golden raisins to the bread machine one by one, according to the manufacturer's instructions.
Select the Bake cycle
Close the lid, select the sweet or basic bread, medium crust setting on your bread machine and press start.
Add the cranberries and golden raisins 5 to 10 minutes before the last kneading cycle ends.
When the bread machine has finished baking, remove the bread and put it on a cooling rack.

Chocolate-pistachio Bread

Servings: 2/3 Cup (24 Slices)

Cooking Time: 10 Minutes

Ingredients:
2/3 cup granulated sugar
½ cup butter, melted
¾ cup milk
1 egg
1½ cups all-purpose flour
cup chopped pistachio nuts
½ cup semisweet chocolate chips
1/3 cup unsweetened baking cocoa
teaspoons baking powder
¼ teaspoon salt
Decorator sugar crystals, if desired

Directions:
Preparing the Ingredients.
Choose the size of loaf of your preference and then measure the ingredients.
Add all of the ingredients mentioned previously in the list. Close the lid after placing the pan in the bread machine.
Select the Bake cycle
Turn on the bread machine. Select the White/Basic setting, select the loaf size, and the crust color. Press start.
When the cycle is finished, carefully remove the pan from the bread maker and let it rest. 7. Remove the bread from the pan, put in a wire rack to cool for at least 2 hours. Wrap tightly and store at room temperature up to 4 days, or refrigerate.

Chia Sesame Bread

Servings: 1 Loaf

Cooking Time: 10 Minutes

Ingredients:
12 slice bread (1½ pounds)
1 cup plus 2 tablespoons water, at 80°F to 90°F
1½ tablespoons melted butter, cooled
1½ tablespoons sugar
1⅛ teaspoons salt
½ cup ground chia seeds
1½ tablespoons sesame seeds
2½ cups white bread flour
1½ teaspoons bread machine or instant yeast

Directions:
Preparing the Ingredients.
Choose the size of loaf of your preference and then measure the ingredients.
Add all of the ingredients mentioned previously in the list.
Close the lid after placing the pan in the bread machine.
Select the Bake cycle
Turn on the bread machine. Select the White/Basic setting, select the loaf size, and the crust color. Press start.
When the cycle is finished, carefully remove the pan from the bread maker and let it rest.
Remove the bread from the pan, put in a wire rack to Cool about 5 minutes. Slice

Oatmeal Sunflower Bread

Servings: 10

Cooking Time: 3 Hours 30 Minutes

Ingredients:
Water – 1 cup.
Honey – ¼ cup.
Butter – 2 tbsps., softened
Bread flour – 3 cups.
Old fashioned oats – ½ cup.
Milk powder – 2 tbsps.
Salt – 1 ¼ tsps.
Active dry yeast – 2 ¼ tsps.
Sunflower seeds – ½ cup.

Directions:
Add all ingredients except for sunflower seeds into the bread machine pan. Select basic setting then select light/medium crust and press start. Add sunflower seeds just before the final kneading cycle. Once loaf is done, remove the loaf pan from the machine. Allow it to cool for 10 minutes. Slice and serve.

Caraway Rye Bread

Servings: 1 Loaf

Cooking Time: 10 Minutes

Ingredients:
12 slice bread (1½ pounds)
1⅛ cups water, at 80°F to 90°F
1¾ tablespoons melted butter, cooled
3 tablespoons dark brown sugar
1½ tablespoons dark molasses
1⅛ teaspoons salt
1½ teaspoons caraway seed
¾ cup dark rye flour
2 cups white bread flour
1⅛ teaspoons bread machine or instant yeast

Directions:
Preparing the Ingredients.
Choose the size of loaf of your preference and then measure the ingredients.
Add all of the ingredients mentioned previously in the list.
Close the lid after placing the pan in the bread machine.
Select the Bake cycle
Turn on the bread machine. Select the White/Basic setting, select the loaf size, and the crust color. Press start.
When the cycle is finished, carefully remove the pan from the bread maker and let it rest. Remove the bread from the pan, put in a wire rack to Cool about 10 minutes. Slice

Honey And Milk White Bread

Servings: 1 Pound Loaf

Cooking Time: 3 Hours

Ingredients:
Lukewarm whole milk :½ cup
Unsalted butter :¾ tbsp
Honey :¾ tbsp
White all-purpose Flour :1 ½ cups
Salt :1 pinch
Bread machine yeast :2/4 tsp

Directions:
Add the ingredients into the bread machine as per the order of the ingredients listed above or follow your bread machine's instruction manual.
Select the white bread function and the light crust function.
When ready, turn the bread out onto a drying rack and allow it to cool, then serve.

Nutrition Info: Calories: 102.5 kcal / Total fat: 1.9 g / Saturated fat: 0.7 g / Cholesterol: 2.4 mg / Total carbohydrates: 18.3 g / Dietary fiber: 0.7 g / Sodium: 202.8 mg / Protein: 2.9 g

Ciabatta

Servings: 1 Pound Loaf

Cooking Time: 30 Minutes

Ingredients:
Lukewarm water :¾ cup
Extra-virgin olive oil :½ tbsp
White all-purpose flour :1 ½ cups
Salt :¾ tsp
Sugar :½ tsp
Bread machine yeast :¾ tsp

Directions:

Add the ingredients into the bread machine as per the order of the ingredients listed above or follow your bread machine's instruction manual.

Select the dough cycle.

When the dough is ready, place it onto a floured surface. Cover the dough with a ceramic or glass dish and allow it to rest for ten minutes. Shape the dough an oval shape. Split into two oval shapes when doubling up on the recipe.

Place onto a greased baking tray, cover with a cloth and allow to rest for a further 30 minutes or until it has doubled in size. Allow the dough to rest in a dry, warm area of your kitchen.

Preheat your oven to 425 °F.

Using the bottom end of a wooden spoon make small indents on the top of each loaf. Drive the spoon down into the dough until it touches the baking tray. Then place into the oven and bake for 30 minutes. Sprinkle water lightly over the top of the loaves every 10 minutes while baking.

When ready, turn the bread out onto a drying rack and allow it to cool, then serve.

Nutrition Info: Calories: 190 kcal / Total fat: 2.2 g / Saturated fat: 0.3 g / Cholesterol: 0 mg / Total carbohydrates: 36.6 g / Dietary fiber: 1.4 g / Sodium: 441 mg / Protein: 5.1 g

Low-carb Bagel

Servings: 12 Pcs

Cooking Time: 25 Minutes

Ingredients:
1 cup protein powder, unflavored
1/3 cup coconut flour
1 tsp. baking powder
½ tsp. sea salt
¼ cup ground flaxseed
1/3 cup sour cream
12 eggs
Seasoning topping:
1 tsp. dried parsley
1 tsp. dried oregano
1 tsp. Dried minced onion
½ tsp. Garlic powder
½ tsp. Dried basil
½ tsp. sea salt

Directions:

Preheat the oven to 350F.

In a mixer, blend sour cream and eggs until well combined.

Whisk together the flaxseed, salt, baking powder, protein powder, and coconut flour in a bowl.

Mix the dry ingredients until it becomes wet ingredients. Make sure it is well blended.

Whisk the topping seasoning together in a small bowl. Set aside.

Grease 2 donut pans that can contain six donuts each.

Sprinkle pan with about 1 tsp. Topping seasoning and evenly pour batter into each.

Sprinkle the top of each bagel evenly with the rest of the seasoning mixture.

Bake in the oven for 25 minutes, or until golden brown.

Nutrition Info: Calories: 134;Fat: 6.8g;Carb: 4.2g;Protein: 12.1

Delicious Sour Cream Bread

Servings: 1 Loaf

Cooking Time: 10 Minutes Plus Fermenting Time

Ingredients:
12 slice bread (1½ pounds)
½ cup + 1 tablespoon lukewarm water
½ cup + 1 tablespoon sour cream, at room temperature
2¼ tablespoons butter, at room temperature
1 tablespoon maple syrup
¾ teaspoon table salt
2¾ cups white bread flour
1⅔ teaspoons bread machine yeast

Directions:
Preparing the Ingredients.
Choose the size of loaf of your preference and then measure the ingredients.
Add all of the ingredients mentioned previously in the list.
Close the lid after placing the pan in the bread machine.
Select the Bake cycle
Turn on the bread machine. Select the Basic/White setting, select the loaf size, and the crust color. Press start.
When the cycle is finished, carefully remove the pan from the bread maker and let it rest.
Remove the bread from the pan, put in a wire rack to Cool about 5 minutes. Slice

Moist Cheddar Cheese Bread

Servings: 10

Cooking Time: 3 Hours 45 Minutes

Ingredients:
Milk – 1 cup
Butter – ½ cup, melted
All-purpose flour – 3 cups
Cheddar cheese – 2 cups, shredded
Garlic powder – ½ tsp.
Kosher salt – 2 tsps.
Sugar – 1 tbsp.
Active dry yeast – 1 ¼ oz.

Directions:
Add milk and butter into the bread pan. Add remaining ingredients except for yeast to the bread pan. Make a small hole into the flour with your finger and add yeast to the hole. Make sure yeast will not be mixed with any liquids. Select basic setting then select light crust and start. Once loaf is done, remove the loaf pan from the machine. Allow it to cool for 10 minutes. Slice and serve.

Apple Honey Bread

Servings: 1 Loaf

Cooking Time: 10 Minutes Plus Fermenting Time

Ingredients:
12 slice bread (1½ pounds)
5 tablespoons lukewarm milk
3 tablespoons apple cider, at room temperature
3 tablespoons sugar
tablespoons unsalted butter, melted
1½ tablespoons honey
¼ teaspoon table salt
cups white bread flour
1¼ teaspoons bread machine yeast
1 apple, peeled, cored, and finely diced

Directions:
Preparing the Ingredients.
Choose the size of loaf of your preference and then measure the
ingredients.
Add all of the ingredients mentioned previously in the list, except for
the apples. Close the lid after placing the pan in the bread machine.
Select the Bake cycle
Turn on the bread maker. Select the White/Basic or Fruit/Nut (if your
machine has this setting) setting, then the loaf size, and finally the crust
color. Start the cycle.
When the machine signals to add ingredients, add the apples. When the
cycle is finished, carefully remove the pan from the bread maker and let
it rest. Remove the bread from the pan, put in a wire rack to Cool
about 5 minutes. Slice

Cinnamon Pull-apart Bread

Servings: 16

Cooking Time: 3 Hours

Ingredients:
1/3 cup whole milk
4 tablespoons unsalted butter
1/4 cup warm water
teaspoon pure vanilla extract
large eggs
cups all-purpose flour
1/4 cup sugar
1/2 teaspoon salt
2 1/4 teaspoons active dry yeast For the Filling:
4 tablespoons unsalted butter, melted until browned (will smell like warm caramel)
cup sugar
teaspoons ground cinnamon
Pinch of ground nutmeg

Directions:

Add milk and butter to a saucepan and heat on medium-low until the butter melts; add liquid to the bread maker. Add the rest of the ingredients (except yeast) in the order listed.

Make a well in the center of the dry ingredients and add the yeast.

Select Dough cycle and press Start. When the dough is done, roll it out into a big sheet of dough, and brush the dough with the browned butter. Combine sugar cinnamon and nutmeg in a mixing bowl and sprinkle over buttered dough.

Cut the dough into long thin strips and cut the strips into squares. Stack in threes, and place the dough squares next to one another in a greased bread pan.

Let rise in a warm place until doubled in size; cover with plastic wrap and refrigerate overnight to bake for breakfast.

Preheat an oven to 350°F. Bake for 30 to 35 minutes, until the top is very golden brown.

When bread is done, transfer to a plate to cool and serve warm.

Nutrition Info: Calories: 210, Sodium: 126 mg, Dietary Fiber: 0.9 g, Fat: 6.8 g, Carbs: 34.3 g, Protein: 3.7 g.

Strawberry Shortcake Bread

Servings: 1 Loaf

Cooking Time: 10 Minutes

Ingredients:
12 slice bread (1½ pounds)
1⅛ cups milk, at 80°F to 90°F
3 tablespoons melted butter, cooled
3 tablespoons sugar
1½ teaspoons salt
¾ cup sliced fresh strawberries
1 cup quick oats
2¼ cups white bread flour
1½ teaspoons bread machine or instant yeast

Directions:
Preparing the Ingredients.
Choose the size of loaf of your preference and then measure the ingredients.
Add all of the ingredients mentioned previously in the list. Close the lid after placing the pan in the bread machine.
Select the Bake cycle
Turn on the bread machine. Select the White/Basic setting, select the loaf size, and the crust color. Press start.
When the cycle is finished, carefully remove the pan from the bread maker and let it rest.
Remove the bread from the pan, put in a wire rack to cool for at least 2 hours, and slice.

Cranberry & Golden Raisin Bread

Servings: 14 Slices

Cooking Time: 10 Minutes

Ingredients:
1⅓ cups water
4 Tbsp sliced butter
3 cups flour
1 cup old fashioned oatmeal
⅓ cup brown sugar
1 tsp salt
4 Tbsp dried cranberries
4 Tbsp golden raisins
2 tsp bread machine yeast

Directions:
Preparing the Ingredients
Add each ingredient except cranberries and golden raisins to the bread machine one by one, according to the manufacturer's instructions.
Select the Bake cycle
Close the lid, select the sweet or basic bread, medium crust setting on your bread machine and press start.
Add the cranberries and golden raisins 5 to 10 minutes before the last kneading cycle ends.
When the bread machine has finished baking, remove the bread and put it on a cooling rack.

Grain, Seed And Nut Bread

Servings: 1 Loaf

Cooking Time: 10 Minutes

Ingredients:
¼ cup water
1 egg
3 Tbsp honey
1½ tsp butter, softened
3¼ cups bread flour
1 cup milk
1 tsp salt
¼ tsp baking soda
1 tsp ground cinnamon
2½ tsp active dry yeast
¾ cup dried cranberries
½ cup chopped walnuts
1 Tbsp white vinegar
½ tsp sugar

Directions:
Preparing the Ingredients.
Choose the size of loaf of your preference and then measure the
ingredients.Add all of the ingredients mentioned previously in the list.
Close the lid after placing the pan in the bread machine.
Select the Bake cycleTurn on the bread machine. Select the
White/Basic setting, select the loaf size, and the crust color. Press start.
When the cycle is finished, carefully remove the pan from the bread
maker and let it rest. 8.   Remove the bread from the pan, put in a wire
rack to Cool about 10 minutes. Slice

Pecan Raisin Bread

Servings: 1 Loaf

Cooking Time: 10 Minutes Plus Fermenting Time

Ingredients:
1 cup plus 2 Tbsp water (70°F to 80°F)
8 tsp butter
1 egg
6 Tbsp sugar
¼ cup nonfat dry milk powder
1 tsp salt
4 cups bread flour
1 Tbsp active dry yeast
1 cup finely chopped pecans
1 cup raisins

Directions:
Preparing the Ingredients
Add each ingredient to the bread machine except the pecans and raisins in the order and at the temperature recommended by your bread machine manufacturer.
Select the Bake cycle
Close the lid, select the basic bread, medium crust setting on your bread machine, and press start.
Just before the final kneading, add the pecans and raisins.
When the bread machine has finished baking, remove the bread and put it on a cooling rack.

Cracked Black Pepper Bread

Servings: 1 Loaf

Cooking Time: 10 Minutes

Ingredients:
12 slice bread (1½ pounds)
1⅛ cups water, at 80°F to 90°F
1½ tablespoons melted butter, cooled
1½ tablespoons sugar
1 teaspoon salt
3 tablespoons skim milk powder
1½ tablespoons minced chives
¾ teaspoon garlic powder
¾ teaspoon freshly cracked black pepper
3 cups white bread flour
1¼ teaspoons bread machine or instant yeast

Directions:
Preparing the Ingredients.
Choose the size of loaf of your preference and then measure the ingredients.
Add all of the ingredients mentioned previously in the list.
Close the lid after placing the pan in the bread machine.
Select the Bake cycle
Turn on the bread machine. Select the White/Basic setting, select the loaf size, and the crust color. Press start.
When the cycle is finished, carefully remove the pan from the bread maker and let it rest.
Remove the bread from the pan, put in a wire rack to Cool about 10 minutes. Slice

Paleo And Dairy-free Bread

Servings: 1 Pound Loaf

Cooking Time: 3 Hours

Ingredients:
Flax meal :¼ cup
Chia seeds :2 tbsp
Coconut oil, melted :⅛ cup
Egg :1 ½
Almond milk :¼ cup
Honey :½ tbsp
Almond flour :1 cup
Tapioca flour :⅔ cup
Coconut flour :⅛ cup
Salt :½ tsp
Cream of tartar :1 tsp
Bread machine yeast :1 tsp

Directions:

In a mixing bowl, combine one tablespoon of flax meal with the chia seeds. Stir in the water and set aside.

In a separate mixing bowl, pour in the melted coconut oil, eggs, almond milk, and honey. Whisk together. Followed by whisking in the flax meal and chia seed mixture. Pour this into the bread machine.

In a mixing bowl, combine the almond, tapioca, and coconut flour. Add the remainder of the flax meal and salt. Add in the cream of tartar and baking soda.

Pour the dry ingredients on top of the wet ingredients.

Finish by adding the yeast.

Select the whole wheat setting and medium crust function.

When ready, turn the bread out onto a drying rack and allow it to cool, then serve.

Nutrition Info: Calories: 142 kcal / Total fat: 6.3 g / Saturated fat:1.8g / Cholesterol: 34.9 mg / Total carbohydrates: 15.5 g / Dietary fiber: 4.4 g / Sodium: 236.8 mg / Protein: 4.1 g

Cinnamon Babaka

Servings: 1 Loaf

Cooking Time: 45 Minutes

Ingredients:
For the Dough
¾ c milk, warmed to 80-90F
2 ¼ tsp (1 packet) active dry yeast
4 Tbsp unsalted butter
3 Tbsp sugar
2 egg yolks (reserve the whites, separately, see below)
tsp pure vanilla extract
eggs (whole)
½ - 4 c unbleached all-purpose flour
1 tsp salt
For the Filling
1 c brown sugar
Tbsp cinnamon
¼ tsp salt
Tbsp unsalted butter melted and cooled
1 egg white (see above)
For the Egg Wash
1 egg white (see above), lightly beate

Directions:

FOR THE DOUGH:

In a small bowl, mix the warmed milk and yeast. Let this mixture to rest aside for 5-10 minutes, until the yeast starts to foam. Meanwhile, cream the butter and sugar together with an electric hand mixer in a medium bowl. Add, one at a time, the egg yolks, while beating them. Set this mixture aside too.

Give the yeast mixture a stir, then add it to the bowl of your bread machine. Add the egg and butter mixture to the milk. Pour the salt and 3 cups of flour.

Start your bread machine on its Dough Cycle. Watch your dough as it begins to knead. Once it looks like the ingredients are completely mixed, add more flour, a ¼ cup at a time, letting the machine knead between each addition, until the dough comes together and pulls away from the sides of the bowl.

When it happens, close your bread machine and let the machine run through its Dough Cycle. When the cycle is done, wait for the bread to become double its size.

FOR THE FILLING:

Now make the filling by whisking all of the filling ingredients together in a medium bowl, until it becomes smooth and then let it set aside.

PUTTING IT ALL TOGETHER

Grease a 9x5 loaf pan and line it with greased parchment paper. 12. Tip the dough out of its rising bowl onto a well-floured surface. Punch the dough down and roll it out into a roughly 18x15 inch rectangle. Spread filling evenly over dough, leaving a 1 inch border on the long sides. Roll the dough, starting from one of the long sides.

Cut the roll in half, lengthwise, turning it into two strands. Twist the two strands together, trying to keep the cut (exposed filling) side on top, as much as possible. Finally, shape your twisted dough into a figure 8, again keeping the cut sides up as much as possible. Place this twisted figure 8 into the greased and lined loaf pan.

Cover the dough in the pan loosely with plastic wrap and let rise for 30 minutes.

After 30 minutes, preheat your oven to 350F. When the dough has risen slightly and looks puffy, remove the plastic wrap and brush the top of the dough with the beaten egg white egg wash. Bake the bread at 350F for 45-55 minutes, until the top crust is deeply golden and the loaf sounds hollow when tapped. (The internal temperature of the loaf should read around 180F when the bread is done). (It may be helpful to place a piece of aluminum foil or an aluminum foil lined baking sheet on the rack under the bread to catch any filling that my bubble out of the loaf.)

Once the loaf is done, cool the bread in the pan for 10 minutes, before gently removing the bread from the pan to continue to cool for 10-20 minutes before slicing.

The babka will stay fresh stored in airtight container at room temperature for up to 3 days, then move the bread to the refrigerator.

Nutrition Info: Calories 219 ; Protein 6.6g; Carbohydrates 32g; Fat: 10.5g

Cheddar Cheese Bread

Servings: 20

Cooking Time: 3 Hours And 25 Minutes

Ingredients:
Water – ¾ cup
Egg – 1
Salt – 1 tsp.
Bread flour – 3 cups
Shredded sharp cheddar cheese – 1 cup
Nonfat dry milk – 2 tbsp.
Sugar – 2 tbsp.
Bread machine yeast – 1 tsp.

Directions:
Add everything according to bread machine recommendations.
Select Basic/White bread and Medium crust.
Remove the bread when done.
Cool, slice, and serve.

Nutrition Info: Calories: 101; Total Fat: 2.3 g; Saturated Fat: 1.3 g; Carbohydrates: 15.8 g; Cholesterol: 15 mg; Fiber: 0.6 g; Calcium: 48 mg; Sodium: 157 mg; Protein: 3.8 g

Mozzarella Cheese And Salami Loaf

Servings: 1 Loaf

Cooking Time: 45 Minutes

Ingredients:
¾ cup water, set at 80 degrees F
1/3 cup mozzarella cheese, shredded
Four teaspoons sugar
2/3 teaspoon salt
2/3 teaspoon dried basil
Pinch of garlic powder
2 cups + 2 tablespoons white bread flour
One teaspoon instant yeast
½ cup hot salami, finely diced

Directions:
Add the listed ingredients to your bread machine (except salami),
following the manufactures instructions. Set the bread machine's
program to Basic/White Bread and the crust type to light. Press Start.
Let the bread machine work and wait until it beeps. This your
indication to add the remaining ingredients at this point, add the
salami. Wait until the remaining bake cycle completes.
Once the loaf is done, take the bucket out from the bread machine and
let it rest for 5 minutes. Gently shake the bucket and remove the loaf,
transfer the loaf to a cooling rack and slice.
Serve and enjoy!

Nutrition Info: Calories: 164 calories; Total Carbohydrate: 28 g ;
Total Fat: 3 g ; Protein: 6 g ; Sugar: 2 g

Feta Oregano Bread

Servings: 1 Loaf

Cooking Time: 10 Minutes Plus Fermenting Time

Ingredients:
8 slice bread (1 pounds)
⅔ cup milk, at 80°F to 90°F
2 teaspoons melted butter, cooled
2 teaspoons sugar
⅔ teaspoon salt
2 teaspoons dried oregano
2 cups white bread flour
1½ teaspoons bread machine or instant yeast
⅔ cup (2½ ounces) crumbled feta cheese

Directions:
Preparing the Ingredients.
Choose the size of loaf of your preference and then measure the ingredients.
Add all of the ingredients mentioned previously in the list.
Close the lid after placing the pan in the bread machine.
Select the Bake cycle
Turn on the bread machine. Select the Quick/Rapid setting, select the loaf size, and the crust color. Press start.
When the cycle is finished, carefully remove the pan from the bread maker and let it rest. 8.   Remove the bread from the pan, put in a wire rack to Cool about 5 minutes. Slice

Orange Bread

Servings: 1 Loaf

Cooking Time: 10 Minutes

Ingredients:
16 slice bread (2 pounds)
1¼ cups lukewarm milk
¼ cup orange juice
¼ cup sugar
1½ tablespoons unsalted butter, melted
1¼ teaspoons table salt
4 cups white bread flour
Zest of 1 orange
1¾ teaspoons bread machine yeast

Directions:
Preparing the Ingredients.
Choose the size of loaf of your preference and then measure the ingredients.
Add all of the ingredients mentioned previously in the list. Close the lid after placing the pan in the bread machine
Select the Bake cycle
Turn on the bread machine. Select the White/Basic setting, select the loaf size, and the crust color. Press start.
When the cycle is finished, carefully remove the pan from the bread maker and let it rest. Remove the bread from the pan, put in a wire rack to cool. Cool completely, about 10 minutes. Slice

Oatmeal-streusel Bread

Servings: 1 Loaf

Cooking Time: 10 Minutes

Ingredients:
Streusel
¼ cup packed brown sugar
¼ cup chopped walnuts, toasted
2 teaspoons ground cinnamon
Bread
cup all-purpose flour
½ cup whole wheat flour
½ cup old-fashioned oats
tablespoons ground flaxseed or flaxseed meal
teaspoon baking powder
½ teaspoon salt
¼ teaspoon baking soda
¾ cup packed brown sugar
2/3 cup vegetable oil
eggs
¼ cup sour cream
2 teaspoons vanilla
½ cup milk
Icing
¾ to 1 cup powdered sugar
tablespoon milk
teaspoons light corn syrup

Directions:

Preparing the Ingredients.

Choose the size of loaf of your preference and then measure the ingredients.

Add all of the ingredients mentioned previously in the list. Close the lid after placing the pan in the bread machine

Select the Bake cycle.

Turn on the bread machine. Select the White/Basic setting, select the loaf size, and the crust color. Press start.

When the cycle is finished, carefully remove the pan from the bread maker and let it rest.

Remove the bread from the pan, put in a wire rack to Cool completely, about 2 hours. In small bowl, beat all icing ingredients, adding enough of the powdered sugar for desired drizzling consistency. Drizzle icing over bread. Let stand until set. Wrap tightly and store at room temperature up to 4 days, or refrigerate. To toast walnuts, bake in ungreased shallow pan at 350°F for 7 to 11 minutes, stirring occasionally, until light brown.

Seeded Bread

Servings: 16 Slices

Cooking Time: 40 Minutes

Ingredients:
Two tablespoons chia seeds
1/4 teaspoon salt
Seven large eggs
1/2 teaspoon xanthan gum
2 cups almond flour
One teaspoon baking powder
1/2 cup unsalted butter
Three tablespoons sesame seeds
Two tablespoons olive oil

Directions:
Add all the ingredients to the Bread machine.
Close the lid and choose Bread mode. Once done, take out from the machine and cut into at least 16 slices.
This seeded bread can be kept for up to 4-5 days in the fridge.

Nutrition Info: Calories: 101 Cal; Fat: 4 g; Cholesterol:;
Carbohydrates: 4 g;Protein: 6 g

Pumpkin Cinnamon Bread

Servings: 14 Slices

Cooking Time: 3 H.

Ingredients:
1 cup sugar
1 cup canned pumpkin
⅓ cup vegetable oil
tsp vanilla
eggs
1½ cups all-purpose bread flour
2 tsp baking powder
¼ tsp salt
1 tsp ground cinnamon
¼ tsp ground nutmeg
⅛ tsp ground cloves

Directions:
Add each ingredient to the bread machine in the order and at the temperature recommended by your bread machine manufacturer. Close the lid, select the quick, medium crust setting on your bread machine and press start.
When the bread machine has finished baking, remove the bread and put it on a cooling rack.

Fragrant Cardamom Bread

Servings: 1 Loaf

Cooking Time: 10 Minutes

Ingredients:
12 slices bread (1½ pounds)
¾ cup milk, at 80°F to 90°F
1 egg, at room temperature
1½ teaspoons melted butter, cooled
3 tablespoons honey
1 teaspoon salt
1 teaspoon ground cardamom
3 cups white bread flour
1¼ teaspoons bread machine or instant yeast

Directions:
Preparing the Ingredients.
Choose the size of loaf of your preference and then measure the ingredients.
Add all of the ingredients mentioned previously in the list.
Close the lid after placing the pan in the bread machine.
Select the Bake cycle
Turn on the bread machine. Select the White/Basic setting, select the loaf size, and the crust color. Press start.
When the cycle is finished, carefully remove the pan from the bread maker and let it rest. 8.   Remove the bread from the pan, put in a wire rack to Cool about 10 minutes. Slice

CPSIA information can be obtained
at www.ICGtesting.com
Printed in the USA
BVHW05032708o521
606757BV00010B/1498